KV-531-232

Contents

List of tables and figures

Divided by Language

*A study of participation and competence in languages
in Great Britain undertaken by NIACE*

Fiona Aldridge

WITHDRAWN
FROM
UNIVERSITY OF PLYMOUTH
LIBRARY SERVICES

NIACE
THE NATIONAL ORGANISATION
FOR ADULT LEARNING

Published by the National Institute of
Adult Continuing Education (England and Wales)

21 De Montfort Street
Leicester LE1 7GE
Company registration no. 2603322
Charity registration no. 1002775

© 2001 National Institute of Adult Continuing Education
(England and Wales)

All rights reserved. No reproduction, copy or transmission
of this publication may be made without the written permission
of the publishers, save in accordance with the provisions of
the Copyright, Designs and Patents Act 1988, or under the
terms of any licence permitting limited copying issued by the
Copyright Licensing Agency.

University of Plymouth
Library

Item No.
90 06332696

Shelfmark
374 ALD

NIACE, the national organisation for adult learning, has a
broad remit to promote lifelong learning opportunities for
adults. NIACE works to develop increased participation in
education and training, particularly for those who do not have
easy access because of barriers of class, gender, age, race,
language and culture, learning difficulties and disabilities, or
insufficient financial resources.

NIACE's website on the Internet is http://www.niace.org.uk

Cataloguing in Publication Data
A CIP record of this title is available from the British Library

ISBN 1 86201 114 1

Foreword

Divided by Language is the product of a project started in 1999 when NIACE carried out a survey of language learning to help provide evidence for the Nuffield Inquiry into modern languages. Language learning is often seen as the backbone of traditional evening class provision and we were keen to see how far it penetrated the population as a whole.

What the survey uncovers is exciting and challenges the view that little learning of languages exists in England and Wales. Among our minority ethnic populations are incredibly successful and adept language learners often with more than two languages at their disposal. Their fluency and ability to embrace language learning stand out in this survey and invite further work on learning strategies and motivation.

Fiona Aldridge has provided us with a clear and thorough piece of work. A picture is drawn from the statistics of a population interested in languages but facing the same difficulties, in terms of getting involved, that confront other forms of adult learning. Being older, poor and of a lower social class all result in less engagement.

As we approach the European Year of Languages we need to take the lessons learned from this study and use them in the promotion, not just of European languages in the European Union, but also of the wealth of language learning being brought into Europe from further afield. This enriches us all and has the capacity to develop the provision we have traditionally made.

Sue Cara
Associate Director

Acknowledgements

Adult Learners' Week is supported by the European Social Fund and Department for Education and Employment. This survey, undertaken as part of the Week, was also supported by the Nuffield Languages Inquiry. NIACE is grateful to Pauline Swanton for her language expertise in the questionnaire design and report writing stages.

Key findings

How many languages?

1. 29% of adults can speak one foreign language, and 13% of adults can speak two or more foreign languages
2. Almost 6 in 10 adults speak only their mother tongue
3. 15% of adults are bilingual
4. Men and women speak as many languages as each other
5. Social class has a major impact upon the number of languages spoken. 65% of ABs speak one or more additional languages compared with 49% of C1s, 34% of C2s and 28% of DEs
6. 45% of adults in work speak more than one language, compared with 39% of those who are unemployed, 34% of those who are retired and 31% of those not in paid employment
7. Full-time students are most likely to have additional language abilities. 76% speak more than one language, 28% speak more than two languages and 32% are bilingual
8. Younger adults speak more languages than older adults. 70% of 16-19-year-olds speak more than one language compared to around 30% of those over 60
9. There are strong regional differences in the numbers of adults speaking additional languages. Wales (52%) and Greater London (51%) have most adults speaking more than one language
10. 49% of adults with a first language other than English speak at least two other languages, compared to 11% of those whose first language is English
11. Britain's black and minority ethnic communities are a rich linguistic resource. 45% speak more than two other languages compared to 11% of white adults

Current participation in language learning

12. Only 5% of adults are currently learning a language
13. People surveyed are learning 21 different languages
14. French, German, Spanish and Italian are the most common languages being learned
15. The same proportion of men and women are currently learning a language (5%)

16. Social class is a key factor in understanding participation in language learning. Those in social classes AB (8%) are twice as likely to be learning a language than those in any other social class (4%)
17. Full-time students (26%) are much more likely to be learning a language than those of any other employment status
18. Participation in language learning is greatest among young adults (22% of 16-19-year-olds), and decreases with age (2% of those over 60)
19. Except for London where 9% of the adult population are currently learning a language, there is little regional variation in language learning participation
20. A greater proportion of Britain's black and ethnic minorities (12%) participate in language learning than its white population (4%)

Future language learning intentions

21. 44% of adults would like to learn a language if they had the time and opportunity
22. People surveyed would like to learn 57 different languages and dialects
23. More women (57%) than men (54%) expressed an interest in learning a language in the future, although more men would like to learn German
24. Those in the highest social classes are most likely to participate in future language learning, therefore participation rates between different classes are likely to widen
25. Full-time students (69%) and those in full-time employment (54%) expressed the greatest interest in learning a language in the future
26. Only a quarter of retired respondents expressed any future intention to learn a language
27. Older adults are less likely to take up language learning in the future. 20% of those over 70 have future intentions to learn a language compared with 60% of 16-19-year-olds
28. Regional differences exist in the number of adults who would like to learn a language in the future. The highest future intentions are expressed in Wales (62%), the North West

(52%), London (49%) and the North (49%)

29. Black and ethnic minorities (49%) and those who speak a mother tongue other than English (51%) expressed greatest intentions to learn a language in the future

French

30. Historically French has been the primary foreign language learned in Britain and continues to maintain this position

31. 26% of respondents said that they could use, understand, speak or communicate in French or had learned it at some time in the past

32. Of those who have some knowledge of French as a foreign language, 42% felt fairly confident in their understanding skills, 41% in their reading skills, 28% in their speaking skills and 22% in their writing skills

33. Around 80% of those who have some knowledge of French as a foreign language felt that they could complete a basic level task in all four skills

34. 30% of those who have some knowledge of French as a foreign language said that they could make sense of the news on television, 42% could cope with a visit to the doctor and 45% could make sense of articles in a newspaper

German

35. Historically German has been the second most popular foreign language learned in Britain and continues to maintain this position, although it is now in decline

36. 10% of respondents said that they could use, understand, speak or communicate in German or had learned it at some time in the past

37. Of those who have some knowledge of German as a foreign language, 41% felt fairly confident in their understanding skills, 34% in their reading skills, 29% in their speaking skills and 17% in their writing skills

38. Around 80% of those who have some knowledge of German as a foreign language felt that they could complete a basic level task in understanding, speaking and reading. Only 68% of respondents felt

confident that they could complete a basic writing task

39. 37% of those who have some knowledge of German as a foreign language said that they could make sense of the news on television, 40% could cope with a visit to the doctor and 41% could make sense of articles in a newspaper

Spanish

40. The number of adults learning Spanish in Britain is growing rapidly with the main motivation being for holiday travel to Spanish speaking destinations

41. 5% of respondents said that they could use, understand, speak or communicate in Spanish or had learned it at some time in the past

42. Of those who have some knowledge of Spanish as a foreign language, 50% felt fairly confident in their understanding skills, 44% in their reading skills, 38% in their speaking skills and 26% in their writing skills

43. A high proportion of those who have some knowledge of Spanish as a foreign language are successful in reaching basic level, especially in understanding (87%), reading (89%) and speaking skills (82%)

44. 44% of those who have some knowledge of Spanish as a foreign language said that they could make sense of the news on television, 52% could cope with a visit to the doctor and 55% could make sense of articles in a newspaper

Italian

45. There has been a recent surge in the number of adults learning Italian, although the numbers are now stabilising and remain quite small. Italian is sometimes learned as a holiday language, and often because of an interest in Italian culture

46. 3% of respondents said that they could use, understand, speak or communicate in Italian or had learned it at some time in the past

47. Of those who have some knowledge of Italian as a foreign language, 48% felt fairly confident in their understanding skills, 42% in their reading skills, 34% in their speaking skills and 19% in their writing skills

48. Around 80% of those who have some knowledge of Italian as a foreign language felt that they could complete a basic level task in all four skills

49. 42% of those who have some knowledge of Italian as a foreign language said that they could make sense of the news on television, 51% could cope with a visit to the doctor and 39% could make sense of articles in a newspaper

South Asian languages

50. Within Great Britain these respondents are unique in that they are the only group of foreign language speakers that consistently put the languages they learn into use

51. 3% of respondents said that they could use, understand, speak or communicate in Hindi, Panjabi or Urdu or had learned them at some time in the past

52. Of those who have some knowledge of Hindi, Panjabi or Urdu as foreign languages, 90% felt fairly confident in their understanding skills, 49% in their reading skills, 79% in their speaking skills and 41% in their writing skills

53. 86% of those who have some knowledge of Hindi, Panjabi or Urdu as foreign languages said that they could make sense of the news on television, 86% could cope with a visit to the doctor and 48% could make sense of articles in a newspaper

Other languages

54. 9% of respondents said that they could use, understand, speak or communicate in other languages (excluding English and Welsh) or had learned them at some time in the past

55. Of those who have some knowledge of other foreign languages (excluding English and Welsh), 47% felt fairly confident in their understanding skills, 37% in their reading skills, 32% in their speaking skills and 19% in their writing skills

56. Between 70 and 80% of respondents feel confident that they can complete basic level tasks in understanding, speaking and writing, and between 35-45% feel confident that they can complete intermediate level tasks in these skills. In general, understanding and speaking skills are stronger than reading and writing skills

57. 38% of those who have some knowledge of other foreign languages (excluding English and Welsh) said that they could make sense of the news on television, 45% could cope with a visit to the doctor and 35% could make sense of articles in a newspaper

Introduction

Adults in Great Britain often display an ambivalence to language acquisition. We see ourselves as a nation of monoglots, when in fact Britain contains many vibrant multilingual communities. This language ability is often denied, frequently because traditional language teaching and learning uses fluency as an indication of competency. Adults who carry the baggage of the fluency model from school days will not yet claim or even recognise that they are able to and do in fact use other languages in their daily lives. In a world where the English language is moving inexorably towards being the *lingua franca*, this traditional definition of competency needs challenging for those whose mother tongue is English. Instead, the ability to interact in a basic way through the medium of another language may become a 21st century indicator of language competency.

NIACE is committed to securing more and different adult learning opportunities and recognises the importance of languages and of mapping what adults can do. This piece of research seemed to be of particular importance when the Nuffield Inquiry was working to establish that adults learn and use languages throughout their lives. NIACE shared the Inquiry's concern that adult language learning might not get enough attention within the Inquiry, its findings and recommendations.

The survey, commissioned to coincide with Adult Learners' Week 1999 and to contribute to the Nuffield Languages Inquiry, was carried out for NIACE, the national organisation for adult learning, by RSGB (Research Surveys of Great Britain), which interviewed a representative sample of 4,000 adults aged 16 and over in all three nations of Great Britain during 28 April-2 May and 5-9 May 1999. The detailed analyses were also carried out for NIACE by RSGB and copies of the full tabulations are available from NIACE on request, for a small fee.

The survey endeavoured to encourage respondents to be honest about their language abilities. However, those of English mother tongue tend to underestimate their skill levels, whereas those who primarily speak community languages tend to be more realistic about their abilities.

The headline findings of this survey have already been published in *Tongue-tied but trying?* (Tuckett and Cara, 1999). This report contains more detailed analyses and commentary than was possible in that summary text.

In May 2000, the Nuffield Language Inquiry published its final report into the UK's capability in languages and what we need to do as a nation to improve it. The Inquiry reported that 'everyday we are confronted by evidence that we live in a shrinking world. The breaking down of international barriers, a process which will move much further and faster in the course of this new century, has placed a premium on our ability to talk to our neighbours in the global village....Capability in other languages in crucially important for a flourishing UK.' (Nuffield, 2000)

The Inquiry concluded that English alone is not enough, and that exclusive reliance on the English language leaves the UK vulnerable and dependent on the linguistic competence and goodwill of others. The report recognised that adults are keen to learn languages but are badly served by an impoverished system and recommended that the government should take strategic responsibility for lifelong language learning in order to ensure the investment, collaboration and consultation needed to respond to the demand and drive up standards.

In order to celebrate and promote languages and language learning, 2001 has been designated as the European Year of Languages. This is timely for the UK following the Nuffield Inquiry. The Year, initiated by the Council of Europe and the European Union, and supported by UNESCO, is a pan-European campaign to encourage language learning and publicise the advantages of understanding and speaking other languages, with an emphasis that it is an enjoyable and pleasurable experience, bringing personal as well as economic benefits.
The four main aims of the Year are:

- to raise awareness of the richness of Europe's linguistic heritage;
- to make the widest possible public aware of the advantages of competence in another language;
- to encourage the lifelong learning of languages; and
- to publicise information about the teaching and learning of languages.

The Centre for Information on Language Teaching and Research (CILT) will be co-ordinating a wide-ranging programme of educational, cultural and popularising activities in the UK.

NIACE hopes that this report will be a useful contribution to the work of the Year.

1 How many languages?

Britain is often perceived as being a nation of monoglots. Evidence shows however, that an extremely wide range of languages are used within Great Britain. For example, the Nuffield Languages Inquiry reported that 307 different languages are spoken by London's schoolchildren alone, ranging from Abe (from the Ivory Coast) to Zulu. Even within our survey of 4,000 respondents, 83 different languages and dialects were identified.

Mother tongue

Respondents were asked about their mother tongue, that is the language they first learned as a child. 94% of respondents were of English mother tongue. Another 49 languages and dialects were also cited:

Arabic	Geordie	Malayalam	Somali
Armenian	German (1%)	Maltese	Spanish
Azerbaijani	Greek	Mandarin	Swiss German
Bengali	Gujarati	Mende	Tamil
Chinese	Hebrew	Nepali	Thai
Cockney	Hindi	Panjabi (1%)	Turkish
Czech	Hungarian	Pashto	Twi
Danish	Ibo	Polish	Urdu
Dutch	Irish	Portuguese	Welsh (1%)
Estonian	Italian	Rajput	Yoruba
French	Japanese	Russian	
Frisian	Korean	Scots	
Gaelic	Latvian	Setswana	

Bilingualism

Respondents were then asked if they were bilingual. The term bilingual refers to people who have effective equal control of two native languages, generally as fluently and comfortably as one another, although the term is sometimes interpreted more loosely to reflect near fluency in a second language. 15% of respondents reported that they were bilingual. 40 second languages and dialects were cited:

Afrikaans	Greek	Latin	Scots
Arabic	Gujarati	Malayan	Shona
Chinese	Hausa	Maltese	Slovak
Dutch	Hebrew	Mandarin	Spanish (1%)
Edo	Hindi	Norwegian	Swahili
English (5%)	Hungarian	Panjabi	Thai
Farsi	Ir	Patois	Turkish
French (4%)	Irish	Polish	Urdu (1%)
Gaelic	Italian	Portuguese	Yiddish
German (1%)	Japanese	Russian	Yoruba

Competence in other languages

Plurilingualism refers to the speaking of several languages, such that the individual possesses a portfolio of language competencies. "To be plurilingual also means that although a person may learn several languages, they do not expect to have complete control over all of them" (Nuffield Foundation, 1998). In addition to those languages in which respondents said they were bilingual, respondents cited 52 other languages and dialects which they can use or understand, speak or communicate or have learned at some time in the past:

Afrikaans	French (21%)	Latin	Romanian
Arabic	Gaelic	Lithuanian	Russian
Cantonese	German (9%)	Makaton	Sign Language
Chamaro	Greek (1%)	Malayan	Spanish (4%)
Chinese	Gujarati	Maltese	Swahili
Danish	Hausa	Mandarin	Tamil
Dominica Creole	Hebrew	Mech	Tongues
Dutch	Hindi (1%)	Nepa	Turkish
English	Indonesian	Norwegian	Twi
Esperanto	Irish	Panjabi	Ukranian
Farsi	Italian (2%)	Patois	Urdu (1%)
Finnish	Japanese	Polish	Vietnamese
Flemish	Krio	Portuguese	Welsh (1%)

Number of languages

Tables 1-7 show the number of languages in which respondents are bilingual, can use or understand, speak or communicate or have learned at any time in the past. As the questionnaire was completed in English, those who speak little or no English are under-represented.[1]

13% of respondents speak two or more languages besides their mother tongue, 29% one other language, while 58% of adults questioned speak only their mother tongue.

Table 1 shows the number of languages that adults in Britain speak, by gender. Men and women speak the same number of languages as each other, although a greater proportion of men are bilingual. Men and women speak roughly the same pattern of languages although slightly more women speak French (27% to 24%) and slightly more men speak German (11% to 9%).

Number of languages, by socio-economic class and employment status

Table 2 shows the number of languages, by socio-economic class. Grades A and B, which make up approximately 13% of the total adult population, include the upper and middle classes. Grade C1, approximately 24% of the population, includes the lower-middle class, often referred to as white collar workers. Grade C2, approximately 30% of the population, consists mainly of skilled manual workers. Grades DE, approximately 33% of the population, consists of the semi- and unskilled working classes and those on the lowest levels of subsistence. A full description of socio-economic class categories are given in appendix 3. However, changes in the nature of work and the labour market mean that these categories are beginning to be re-thought.

---

1 NIACE recognises the bias this introduces to the findings. Research undertaken by the Institute of Education and Mori have estimated that almost half a million people whose first language is not English have little command of the English language. (Basic Skills Agency, 1996)

Table 1: **Number of languages, men and women compared**

	Total	Men	Women
Base: all respondents = 100%	4,000	1,870	2,130
Mother tongue only	58	57	59
1 other language	29	29	29
2 other languages	10	10	10
3 other languages	2	3	2
4 other languages	1	1	*
5+ other languages	*	*	*
Bilingual	15%	17%	12%

* represents less than 1% in all the tables in this document
Figures in all tables are rounded to the nearest whole percentage point

Table 2: **Number of languages, by socio-economic class**

	Total	AB	C1	C2	DE
Base: all respondents = 100%	4,000	644	1,173	897	1,286
Mother tongue only	58	35	51	66	72
1 other language	29	42	33	26	20
2 other languages	10	16	12	7	6
3 other languages	2	4	3	1	2
4 other languages	1	1	1	–	*
5+ other languages	*	1	*	-	–
Bilingual	15%	22%	16%	11%	12%

Socio-economic class has a major impact upon the number of languages spoken. 65% of the upper and middle classes (ABs) speak more than one language compared with 49% of the skilled-working class (C1s), 34% of the unskilled working class (C2s) and 28% of people on limited incomes (DEs). French and German are the most common additional languages for all socio-economic classes.

A similar pattern exists for those who are bilingual, although there is less difference between those in classes C2 and DE. 22% of ABs are bilingual, compared with 16% of C1s, 11% of C2s and 12% of DEs.

Table 3 shows the number of languages, by employment status. Those who are classified as being unemployed must be actively seeking work and be on the unemployment register, otherwise they are classified as being not in paid employment.

Employment status also impacts upon the number of languages spoken. 45% of those in employment speak more than one language, compared with 39% of those who are unemployed, 34% of those who are retired and 31% of those who are not in paid employment. There is no difference in the number of languages spoken between those who work full-time and those who work part-time.

Employment status has less impact on bilingualism. 16% of those in part-time employment are bilingual compared with 15% of those in full-time employment and those who are

Table 3: **Number of languages, by employment status**

	Total	Full-time employment	Part-time employment	Unemployed	Not in paid employment	Retired	Full-time student
Base: all respondents = 100%	4,000	1,513	539	169	554	1,006	219
Mother tongue only	58	55	55	61	69	66	24
1 other language	29	31	31	28	21	25	48
2 other languages	10	11	11	8	8	6	21
3 other languages	2	2	3	2	2	2	6
4 other languages	1	1	–	–	–	1	–
5+ other languages	*	*	1	1	–	*	*
Bilingual	15%	15%	16%	15%	9%	13%	32%

unemployed. 13% of those who are retired are bilingual, as are 9% of those who are currently not in paid employment.

Full-time students (at school or in further or higher education) are most likely to have additional language abilities. 76% speak more than one language, 28% speak more than two languages and 32% are bilingual.

French is the most commonly spoken additional language among adults in all categories of employment status. German is the second most common additional language with the highest proportion of its speakers being full time students.

Number of languages, by age group

As Table 4 shows, the older the person, the fewer languages they are, or have at one time been able to speak. 70% of those aged 16-19 speak more than one language. This decreases to 50% for the next age bracket (20-29) and then continues to decline at a more steady rate.

Bilingualism is also greatest among the 16-19 age group (28%), falling to 17% of 20-29 year olds and then decreasing steadily, with a slight increase in the proportion of those aged over 70 (See Figure 1). French and German are the most common additional languages among all age groups.

Table 4: **Number of languages, by age group**

	Total	16-19	20-29	30-39	40-49	50-59	60-69	70+
Base: all respondents = 100%	4,000	274	578	824	611	608	547	558
Mother tongue only	58	30	50	58	58	61	69	68
1 other language	29	49	31	29	28	27	23	23
2 other languages	10	18	14	9	11	9	6	6
3 other languages	2	3	3	3	2	3	1	2
4 other languages	1	–	*	*	1	*	1	1
5+ other languages	*	*	1	*	*	*	*	–
Bilingual	15%	28%	17%	15%	13%	12%	10%	13%

Figure 1: **Bilingualism, by age group**

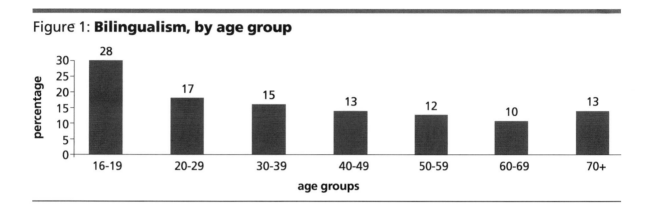

Number of languages, by nation

Comparisons between the three nations of Great Britain (Table 5) reveal considerable differences. 42% of adults in England speak more than one language, compared with 52% in Wales and 31% in Scotland. The Welsh figures are explained in part by the 37% of respondents who speak both English and Welsh. 34% of the Welsh population describe themselves as being bilingual, compared to 14% of the English population and 8% of the Scottish population.

The high Welsh figures can be attributed to the national priority that is given to learning the Welsh language. Local Education Authorities in Wales were first allowed to open Welsh-medium schools following the Education Act of 1944. These schools initially catered for children for whom Welsh was their first language, but by 1960 increasing numbers of pupils came from non-Welsh speaking homes. In 1988, Welsh was included in the National Curriculum and became a compulsory subject for all pupils in Wales at Key Stages 1, 2 and 3 in 1990. In 1999 Welsh became a compulsory subject at Key Stage 4. All pupils in Wales now study Welsh as either a first or second language from the age of five to 16. As a result of this legislation increasingly more adults are emerging from full-time education being able to communicate in Welsh and are also being encouraged to take up the language as adults in order to support their children's learning.

In 1993 the Welsh Language Act placed a duty on the public sector to treat English and Welsh on an equal basis when providing services to the public in Wales. This legislative change, combined with an increased emphasis on Welsh in the workplace, has resulted in increasing awareness of the value of bilingual education, encouraging both the demand for and supply of Welsh provision.

Table 5: **Number of languages, by nation**

	Total	England	Scotland	Wales
Base: all respondents =100%	4,000	3,220	360	204
Mother tongue only	58	58	69	48
1 other language	29	29	25	36
2 other languages	10	10	5	10
3 other languages	2	2	1	5
4 other languages	1	*	*	1
5+ other languages	*	*	–	–
Bilingual	15%	14%	8%	34%

In England, French (26%) and German (10%) are the most common additional languages. In Wales, English (19%), French (18%) and Welsh (18%) are the most common additional languages. In Scotland, French (20%) is the most common additional language.

Number of languages, by region

Comparisons between English regions (Table 6) show a rough north-south divide, ranging from 51% of adults in London to 37% of adults in Yorkshire & Humberside and the North being able to speak more than one language. The number of languages spoken by people living within a particular region is strongly determined by the diversity of communities within the region, the range of provision available and the affluence of the region. For example, the high concentration of multi-ethnic and multi-linguistic communities in the London boroughs contributes strongly to the above figures.

29% of adults living in London are bilingual, as are 16% of those who live in the South East. In the remaining regions, between 8% and 12% of the population are bilingual. East Anglia, Yorkshire and Humberside and the North West have the smallest proportion of bilingual adults.

French is the most common additional language in each of the English regions. In all regions except London, where English is the second most common additional language, German is the next most common.

Number of languages, by mother tongue and ethnicity

62% of adults whose mother tongue is English, speak no other languages and only 10% speak more than one other language (Table 7). 10% of this group are bilingual, with 4% having French as their second language.

People whose mother tongue is not English represent a rich linguistic resource. Only 6% of respondents whose mother tongue is not English speak only that language, with 45% speaking more than one other language. 90% of this group are bilingual, with 81% having English as their second language.

61% of white adults speak only their mother tongue, and only 13% speak more than one other language. 11% are bilingual. French (26%) is the most common additional language.

Non-white adults, especially those of Indian, Bangladeshi or Pakistani origin, represent an

---

Table 6: **Number of languages, by English region**

	Total	London	South East	South West	East Anglia	West Mids	East Mids	North West	Yorkshire/ Humber	North
Base: all respondents = 100%	4,000	492	776	340	148	372	288	452	352	216
Mother tongue only	58	49	59	56	59	63	60	58	59	63
1 other language	29	31	28	32	31	27	26	30	27	26
2 other languages	10	15	9	9	9	7	12	10	11	9
3 other languages	2	4	2	2	2	3	2	2	2	1
4 other languages	1	1	1	1	–	*	*	–	*	*
5+ other languages	*	1	*	–	–	*	*	–	–	–
Bilingual	15%	29%	16%	10%	8%	11%	12%	9%	9%	11%

Caution is needed over the findings relating to East Anglia, which are subject to 2% error in either direction

Table 7: **Number of languages, by mother tongue and ethnicity**

	Mother Tongue			Ethnicity			
	Total	English	Other	White	Black	Indian/ Bangladeshi/ Pakistani	Other
Base: all respondents = 100%	4,000	3,745	245	3,771	64	65	88
Mother tongue only	58	62	06	61	43	1	11
1 other language	29	28	45	28	38	33	41
2 other languages	10	8	33	9	16	41	30
3 other languages	2	2	13	2	3	21	15
4 other languages	1	*	2	*	–	2	2
5+ other languages	*	*	1	*	–	2	1
Bilingual	15%	10%	90%	11%	35%	99%	78%

Figures in all tables are rounded to the nearest whole percent

extremely rich linguistic resource. 18% of non-white adults speak only their mother tongue and 72% are bilingual. When we exclude black adults from these statistics, 7% of respondents speak only their mother tongue and 88% are bilingual. As the sample size of the black and minority ethnic groups is small, these figures may not be representative of the total population.

French (22%) and English (19%) are the most common additional languages for black adults. English (86%), Hindi (36%) and Urdu (29%) are the most common additional languages for Indian, Bangladeshi and Pakistani adults. English (72%) and Urdu (31%) are the most common additional languages for Asian adults.

The table above clearly demonstrates where the majority of Britain's language abilities lie. However, this data needs to be approached with some caution as the table does not compare like with like. Adults whose mother tongue is not English and who are permanent residents of Great Britain are more likely to be bilingual (in their mother tongue and English), in order to participate fully in society.

Adults whose mother tongue is English do not need to be bilingual, although many have survival language competence (for example) coping when on holiday abroad). English speakers tend not to identify this level as 'speaking another language' as many have been brought up to believe that this means becoming fluent.

2 Current participation in language learning

Although 42% of the population can use or understand, speak or communicate, or have learned at any time in the past a language other than their mother tongue, only 5% of adults say that they are currently learning a language. This compares with 22% of the population who reported, in a national participation survey also undertaken by NIACE in 1999, that they were currently participating in 'any form of learning'.

Altogether, respondents are learning 21 different languages and dialects. The most popular were French (65 learners – 2%), Spanish (36 learners – 1%), German (26 learners – 1%) and Italian (15 learners). Other languages were:

Anglo Saxon	English	Portuguese
Arabic	Gaelic	Russian
Bulgarian	Japanese	Sign Language
Cantonese	Latin	Urdu
Chinese	New Testament Greek	Welsh
Dutch	Norwegian	

Table 8 shows that roughly the same proportion of men and women are learning a language, even though the number of men that participate in 'any form of learning' (24%) is slightly higher than the number of women (21%).

Table 8: **Participation in language learning, men and women compared**

	Total	Men	Women
Base: all respondents = 100%	4,000	1,870	2,130
None	95	95	95
French	2	2	2
German	1	1	*
Spanish	1	1	1
Other	1	1	1
Participation in any learning	22%	24%	21%

Participation in language learning, by socio-economic class and employment status

Table 9 shows participation in language learning by socio-economic class. Although there is a strong positive relationship between socio-economic class and participation in 'any learning', the same pattern does not exist in language learning. The proportion of adults in classes AB learning languages (8%) is double that of any other class with the proportion of those learning languages in classes C1, C2, and DE equal at 4%. Those in classes AB are also likely to be learning a wider variety of languages.

Table 9: **Participation in language learning, by socio-economic class**

	Total	AB	C1	C2	DE
Base: all respondents = 100%	4,000	644	1,173	897	1,286
None	95	92	96	96	96
French	2	2	2	2	2
German	1	1	1	1	*
Spanish	1	2	*	1	1
Other	1	4	1	*	1
Participation in any learning	22%	33%	32%	17%	12%

Table 10: **Participation in language learning, by employment status**

	Total	Full-time employment	Part-time employment	Unemployed	Not in paid employment	Retired	Full-time student
Base: all respondents = 100%	4,000	1,513	539	169	554	1,006	219
None	95	96	96	95	98	97	74
French	2	1	1	2	*	1	14
German	1	*	1	–	–	1	4
Spanish	1	1	1	1	1	*	5
Other	1	1	2	2	1	1	5
Participation in any learning	22%	26%	29%	14%	14%	9%	all

As Table 10 shows, there is surprisingly little variation in the proportion of adults who participate in language learning when classified by employment status. Students in full-time education, 26% of whom are currently learning languages, are the only group that show a notably different rate of participation, particularly in French, German and Spanish. Participation in 'any form of learning' is usually found to be strongly related to a person's employment status as it influences their opportunities for learning at work as well as their motivation to learn and the resources available to fund learning.

Participation in language learning, by age group
Generally, the older people are, the less likely they are to participate in 'any form of learning'. As Table 11 shows, with the exception of those in the 40-49 age bracket who participate in lower numbers than we might expect, this relationship also exists when referring to participation in language learning. Those aged between 16-19 are much more likely to participate in language learning than those in any other age group, although participation within this age group is in decline.

Among older adults, learning a language is sometimes perceived as an academic pursuit, a challenge and a means of keeping the brain active. Its academic image, however, can also prove to be a barrier for those with poor previous experiences of formal learning. Older adults, especially the more elderly, may travel abroad less frequently and are therefore less likely to make practical use of languages learned.

Table 11: **Participation in language learning, by age group**

	Total	16-19	20-29	30-39	40-49	50-59	60-69	70+
Base: all respondents = 100%	4,000	274	578	824	611	608	547	558
None	95	78	94	97	95	97	98	98
French	2	13	1	1	1	*	*	1
German	1	4	1	*	*	*	1	*
Spanish	1	3	1	*	1	1	1	–
Other	1	3	3	1	2	1	1	1

Table 12: **Participation in language learning, by nation**

	Total	England	Scotland	Wales
Base: all respondents = 100%	4,000	3,436	360	204
None	95	95	96	95
French	2	2	2	–
German	1	1	*	1
Spanish	1	1	*	–
Welsh	*	–	–	4
Other	1	1	1	–
Participation in any learning	22%	23%	18%	28%

Participation in language learning, by nation and region

Although considerable differences exist between national participation rates in 'any learning', participation rates for the three nations of Great Britain in language learning are very similar (Table 12). Differences do exist, however, in the languages which are learned. In Wales, 4% of respondents are learning Welsh while none of the respondents are learning French or Spanish, the two most popular languages overall.

Participation in 'any learning' also varies by English region. The North and the West Midlands, both of which have been badly hit by the decline in manufacturing, are at the bottom of the list. The highest participation rates exist in East Anglia and the East Midlands.

There is less variation, however, in language learning participation rates between the English regions (Table 13), except for London where 9% of the adult population are learning a language. The regions at the bottom of the list are the South East, the North and the North West where only 3% of the adult population are learning a language.

Table 13: **Participation in language learning, by English region**

	Total	London	South East	South West	East Anglia	West Mids	East Mids	North West	Yorkshire/ Humber	North
Base: all respondents = 100%	4,000	492	776	340	148	372	288	452	352	216
None	95	91	97	95	95	95	96	97	96	97
French	2	2	1	2	2	2	2	1	1	2
German	1	1	1	1	–	*	*	1	–	1
Spanish	1	2	*	1	–	2	–	1	2	–
Other	1	3	1	1	3	1	1	*	1	*
Participation in any learning	22	26	23	23	27	16	27	20	23	17

Caution is needed over the findings relating to East Anglia, which are subject to 2% error in either direction

Participation in language learning, by mother tongue and ethnicity

Table 14 shows participation in language learning, by mother tongue and ethnicity. 4% of those whose mother tongue is English are learning a language, compared to 9% of those of 'other' mother tongues. The majority of this difference is made up of adults who are learning English as an additional language.

The table also shows that a much smaller proportion of white than non-white adults participate in language learning, although the small sample sizes of the black and minority ethnic groups, mean that figures may not be representative of the total population. Spanish and French are the most popular languages being studied by adults from black and minority ethnic groups.

Table 14: **Participation in language learning, by mother tongue and ethnicity**

	Mother Tongue			Ethnicity			
	Total	English	Other	White	Black	Indian/ Bangladeshi/ Pakistani	Other
Base: all respondents = 100%	4,000	3,745	245	3,771	64	65	88
None	95	96	91	96	89	85	59
English	*	–	4	*	1	4	1
French	2	2	1	2	1	6	–
German	1	1	–	1	3	–	–
Spanish	1	1	1	1	5	–	5
Other	•	•	1	1	3	3	2

3 Future language learning intentions

Although only 5% of adults are currently learning a language, it is encouraging that 44% said that they would like to if they had the time and the opportunity.

While our data does not allow us to identify what proportion of the 44% are currently learning a language or involved in some other kind of learning, the NIACE series of participation surveys shows that those most likely to undertake learning in the future are currently or have recently been involved in learning. Past learners and those who have not being involved in learning since leaving full-time education are much less likely to undertake future learning. (see Table 15).

Table 15: Future intentions to learn, by learning status

	Total	Current learners	Recent learners	Past learners	None since full-time
Base: all respondents = 100%	5,054	1,125	919	1,148	1,815
Likely	38	76	60	25	12
Unlikely	59	20	37	72	87
Don't know	3	4	4	2	2

(Source: Sargant, 2000)

Respondents identified the following range of 57 languages and dialects that they would like to learn if they had the time and opportunity:

Afrikaans
Albanian
American
Arabic
Basque
Bengali
Cantonese
Chinese (1%)
Cornish
Croatian
Cypriot
Dominica Creole
Dutch
English
Esperanto
Farsi
Finnish
French (15%)
Gaelic
German (9%)
Ghanaian
Greek (1%)
Hebrew
Hieroglyphics
Hindi
Html
Indonesian
Irish
Italian (7%)
Japanese (2%)
Latin
Malaysian
Mandarin
Maouri
Mexican
Musim
Native American
Norwegian
Pakistani
Panjabi
Polish
Portuguese
Romanian
Russian (1%)
Serbian
Sign language
Spanish (12%)
Swahili
Swedish
Swiss German
Thai
Tibetan
Turkish
Ukrainian
Urdu
Vietnamese
Welsh (2%)

Some respondents would like to learn more than one language, therefore totals exceed 100%.

Table 16: **Future intentions to take up language learning, men and women compared**

	Total	Men	Women
Base: all respondents = 100%	4,000	1,870	2,130
None	56	54	57
French	15	16	15
Spanish	12	12	12
German	9	11	7
Italian	7	6	7
Other	10	12	9
Don't know	3	3	2

54% of men and 57% of women said that they would like to learn a language if they had the time and opportunity (Table 16). Roughly equal proportions of men and women would like to learn French, Spanish and Italian. More men than women are interested in learning German, which may reflect the use of the language for business as well as its anecdotal reputation of appealing to men.

Future intentions, by socio-economic class and employment status

Table 17 shows the future intentions of respondents to take up language learning, by socio-economic class. The evidence shows that in the highest socio-economic classes are most likely to participate in language learning in the future and therefore that participation rates between different classes are likely to widen. Spanish is the most popular choice of language for respondents in classes AB. This may reflect greater opportunities for foreign travel or a deliberate selection of a language other than French or German which may have been learned at another time. French is the most popular language in all other classes.

As Table 18 shows, full-time students (69%), followed by those in full-time employment (54%) expressed the greatest interest in learning a language in the future. Only a quarter of retired respondents expressed any future intention to learn a language.

French is the most popular choice of language for all employment groups except full-time students, for whom Spanish is the most popular choice (26%), followed by French (17%) and

Table 17: **Future intentions to take up language learning, by socio-economic class**

	Total	AB	C1	C2	DE
Base: all respondents = 100%	4,000	644	1,173	897	1,286
None	56	48	51	56	64
French	15	16	19	14	12
Spanish	12	17	13	12	8
German	9	12	8	11	7
Italian	7	10	8	5	4
Other	10	13	12	8	9
Don't know	3	1	2	2	4

Table 18: **Future intentions to take up language learning, by employment status**

	Total	Full-time employment	Part-time employment	Unemployed	Not in paid employment	Retired	Full-time student
Base: all respondents = 100%	4,000	1,513	539	169	554	1,006	219
None	56	46	56	54	56	76	31
French	15	19	14	20	17	8	17
Spanish	12	15	13	12	9	6	26
German	9	13	5	8	8	6	7
Italian	7	7	9	6	6	3	16
Other	10	13	8	9	11	6	17
Don't know	3	2	4	4	4	1	4

then Italian (16%). Of those who expressed an interest in learning German, the highest proportion of respondents were in full-time employment. Respondents in full-time education expressed interest in learning the widest variety of languages.

Future intentions, by age group

Figure 2 shows that the older the respondent, the less likely they are to take up language learning in the future. 60% of 16-19-year-olds would like to learn a language in the future compared to only 20% of those over 70.

Figure 2: **Bilingualism, by age group**

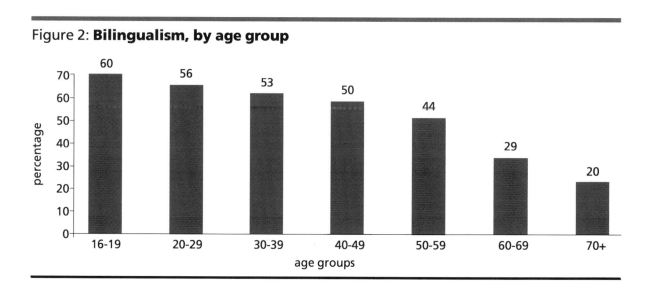

Table 19: **Future intentions to take up language learning, by age group**

	Total	16-19	20-29	30-39	40-49	50-59	60-69	70+
Base: all respondents = 100%	4,000	274	578	824	611	608	547	558
None	56	40	44	47	50	56	71	80
French	15	9	18	22	18	17	10	7
Spanish	12	24	15	14	13	11	9	3
German	9	8	9	10	14	11	5	5
Italian	7	14	11	7	7	5	4	2
Other	10	11	17	12	10	9	6	5
Don't know	3	5	4	3	2	2	2	1

French is the most popular choice of language for all age groups except 16-19-year-olds, for whom Spanish (24%) and then Italian (14%) are the most popular choices (see Table 19). Of those who expressed an interest in learning German, the highest proportion of respondents were aged 40-59. Respondents aged between 20-29 expressed interest in learning the widest variety of languages. Is the younger generation rebelling against historical preponderance of French/German? Are they travelling more?

Future intentions, by nation and region

While current language participation rates in the three nations of Great Britain are all similar (see Table 12), there are greater differences in the proportions of adults who would like to learn a language in the future (Table 20). 62% of respondents living in Wales said that they would like to learn a language, compared with 44% of respondents living in England and 37% of respondents living in Scotland. French and Spanish are the most popular choices of language in England and Scotland. French and Welsh are the most popular choices in Wales.

With the exception of London, there is little variation in current language participation rates between English regions (see Table 13). Greater regional differences exist in future intentions to learn a language (Table 21). Future intentions are greatest in London, the North and the North West and least in South West and Yorkshire and Humberside. These figures are

Table 20: **Future intentions to take up language learning, by nation**

	Total	England	Scotland	Wales
Base: all respondents = 100%	4,000	3,436	360	204
None	56	56	63	38
French	15	15	12	22
Spanish	12	12	13	13
German	9	9	9	10
Italian	7	7	6	6
Welsh	2	1	–	21
Other	9	9	8	5
Don't know	3	3	1	3

Table 21: **Future intentions to take up language learning, by English region**

	Total	London	South East	South West	East Anglia	West Mids	East Mids	North West	Yorkshire/ Humber	North
Base: all respondents = 100%	4,000	492	776	340	148	372	288	452	352	216
None	56	51	57	65	61	57	56	48	65	51
French	15	17	15	14	15	14	15	19	12	15
Spanish	12	14	10	7	11	10	11	17	14	14
German	9	6	11	8	8	10	12	7	6	13
Italian	7	10	7	5	7	6	5	6	5	6
Other	10	13	9	9	3	9	16	10	6	6
Don't know	3	2	2	3	4	2	2	5	1	5

Caution is needed over the findings relating to East Anglia, which are subject to 2% error in either direction

particularly encouraging for the North and North West regions who currently have the lowest language participation rates. French is the most popular choice of language in all regions except Yorkshire and Humberside, where Spanish is the most popular choice. Italian is a favourite choice in London, and German is a favourite in the North, the South East and the Midlands, influenced in part by business concerns.

Future intentions, by mother tongue and ethnicity

Table 22 shows the future intentions of respondents to take up language learning, by mother tongue and ethnicity. Respondents of English mother tongue expressed less interest in learning a language in the future than those of 'other' mother tongues. Respondents of Indian, Bangladeshi and Pakistani origin expressed the greatest interest in learning a language, identifying a wider variety of languages they would like to learn.

Table 22: **Future intentions to take up language learning, by mother tongue and ethnicity**

		Mother Tongue			Ethnicity		
	Total	English	Other	White	Black	Indian/ Bangladeshi/ Pakistani	Other
Base: all respondents = 100%	4,000	3,745	245	3,771	64	65	88
None	56	56	49	57	40	42	49
French	15	15	21	15	25	19	23
Spanish	12	12	11	12	16	8	15
German	9	9	7	9	10	10	6
Italian	7	6	11	6	14	–	17
English	*	–	2	–	–	6	1
Other	10	10	13	10	14	22	10
Don't know	3	3	2	3	2	2	2

Number of languages, current participation and future participation: issues raised
When we bring together the data on the number of languages that adults currently speak, current participation and future intentions to participate in language learning, two main issues emerge.

First, it becomes clear that language ability is not evenly spread among the population, nor are current language learners representative of the population as a whole. Instead, certain groups of the population are more likely to possess language skills than others, with black and minority ethnic adults and adults of 'other' mother tongues representing a rich, linguistic resource.

Those most likely to speak a range of languages are young, in the highest social classes, and in full-time employment. Those least likely to have any foreign language skills are older, in the lowest social classes and are retired, unemployed or not in paid employment.

The inequality of this situation means that despite a national policy emphasis on social inclusion and widening participation, significant proportions of the population are still excluded from the benefits that language competency brings. When we add to this picture respondents' future intentions to learn, our survey shows that participation in language learning appears to be becoming an increasingly elitist activity.

Second, French German, Spanish and Italian are historically the four main foreign languages learned in Great Britain, and our survey confirms that this pattern still continues. Is it appropriate, however, in the light of the diversity of the British population and the globalisation of the economy, for these four languages to remain the main focus of provision or should educational institutions be making a greater case for the broadening of the languages curriculum?

4 French

Historically, French has been the primary foreign language learned in Britain, and continues to maintain this position relatively unquestioned. Modern foreign languages have been widely taught in secondary education for many years and are now part of the national curriculum. Within schools, French is the most commonly taught modern foreign language. For example in 1997, 338,000 English and Welsh students took GCSE French, compared with 136,000 taking GCSE German, 45,000 taking GCSE Spanish and 6,000 taking GCSE Italian. As a result, an increasing proportion of the adult population have some past experience of learning the French language, and will often choose to take up French again if they decide they would like to learn a language in the future.

Throughout Britain, a wide range of French provision for adults is available. This reflects demand for French tuition, possibly fuelled by historical factors and the relative ease with which tutors of French can be located. It also demonstrates a conservatism among learners and providers which favours old friends and fights shy of a broader languages curriculum. In this context, it is interesting to note the popularity of French among black and ethnic minority groups, indicating that communities that have become established in Britain have also linked into this historical tradition.

Competence in French

1,028 of the 4,000 respondents surveyed (26%) said that they could use, understand, speak or communicate in French or had learned it at some time in the past. Of these, 10 said that French was their mother tongue and a further 163 said that they were bilingual in the language. The survey then explored the language competence of the remaining 855.

Only a very a small proportion of the 855 respondents felt confident in their ability to understand, speak, read or write fluently or very well in French. Respondents felt most confident in their ability to understand (42%) and read (41%) the French language at least fairly well and least confident in being able to speak (28%) or write it (22%).

Respondents who have learned through grammatical approaches will have built up considerable competencies in reading and writing skills. Those who have benefited from 'communicative' tuition will have stronger abilities in oral/aural skills. Adult language learning generally takes speaking and understanding as its focus in contact time. Constraints on time available to learn may mean that at the end of the learning period a learner will have achieved uneven levels of ability across the language skills.

Table 23: Competence in French

	Understanding	Speaking	Reading	Writing
Base: all adults who can use, understand, speak or communicate in French as a foreign language = 855 = 100%				
Fluent	1	1	1	*
Very well	3	2	5	2
Fairly well	38	25	35	20
Not very well	54	66	46	57
Not at all	4	6	13	21

Table 24: **Understanding, speaking, reading and writing in French**

	Yes	No	Don't know
Base: all adults who can use, understand, speak or communicate in French as a foreign language = 855 = 100%			
Understanding			
Can you make sense of simple directions?	84	14	2
Can you make sense of the news on television?	30	65	4
Can you understand more or less anything that is said to you?	29	69	2
Speaking			
Can you ask to buy something?	80	18	2
Can you cope with a visit to the doctor?	42	55	3
Can you join in a friendly informal conversation?	18	80	2
Reading			
Can you make sense of common signs?	84	13	3
Can you make sense of articles in newspapers?	45	52	3
Can you understand everything that you read?	12	87	1
Writing			
Can you write a list of words?	78	21	1
Can you string together a simple sentence?	80	19	1
Can you write about more or less anything?	12	88	*

Table 24 explores the competence of respondents who can understand or communicate in French as a foreign language by asking them to identify whether they are able to complete specific tasks at basic, intermediate and advanced levels.

Around 80% of all adults who can use, understand, speak or communicate in French as a foreign language said that they could complete the basic-level task in all four skills. Slightly more respondents felt able to complete the understanding and reading task with fewest respondents feeling able to complete the writing task.

Respondents showed greater variability in the strength of their skills at intermediate level. Only 30% felt confident that they could make sense of the news on television while over 40% felt confident that they could complete the speaking and reading tasks. The question concerning the intermediate writing task needs to be approached with some caution. It was originally designed to represent an intermediate level task. However most respondents interpreted this as less complex than intended and therefore a greater proportion (80%) felt that they would be able to complete it.

At an advanced level, 29% of respondents felt able to complete the understanding task, while less than 20% were able to complete any other task. Respondents were least able to complete the reading and writing tasks.

5 German

Historically, German has been the second most popular foreign language learned in Britain, and currently maintains this position, although is now in decline. German has limited appeal for holiday travel, is still useful in the business context and continues to hold a place in the hearts of learners for historical reasons. The decline in interest in German is difficult to explain satisfactorily but may be due in part to a combination of changing emphases in European economic activity, the decline of second language learning in schools and resultant shortage of German language teachers in all sectors.

Competence in German

417 of the 4,000 respondents surveyed (10%) said that they could use, understand, speak or communicate in German or had learned it at some time in the past. Of these, 21 said that German was their mother tongue and a further 56 said that they were bilingual in the language. The survey explored the language competence of the remaining 340.

Again only a small proportion of the 340 respondents felt confident in their ability to understand, speak, read or write fluently or very well in German. Respondents felt most confident in their ability to understand (41%) the German language and least confident in writing it (17%). 34% felt at least fairly confident in reading the language and 29% in speaking it.

Table 25: **Competence in German**

	Understanding	Speaking	Reading	Writing
Base: all adults who can use, understand, speak or communicate in German as a foreign language = 340 = 100%				
Fluent	1	1	*	*
Very well	4	4	5	3
Fairly well	36	24	29	14
Not very well	55	64	49	54
Not at all	4	8	18	28

Table 26 explores the competence of respondents who can understand or communicate in German as a foreign language by asking them to identify whether they are able to complete specific tasks at basic, intermediate and advanced levels.

Around 80% of all adults who can use, understand, speak or communicate in German as a foreign language said that they could complete the basic level task in understanding, speaking and reading Only 68% of respondents felt confident that they could complete the basic writing task.

Around 40% of respondents said that they could complete the intermediate level task in understanding, speaking and reading. The question concerning the intermediate writing task needs to be approached with some caution. It was originally designed to represent an intermediate level task, however most respondents interpreted this as less complex than intended and therefore a greater proportion (71%) felt that they would be able to complete it.

Table 26: **Understanding, speaking, reading and writing in German**

	Yes	No	Don't know
Base: all adults who can use, understand, speak orn communicate in German as a foreign language = 340 = 100%			
Understanding			
Can you make sense of simple directions?	81	17	2
Can you make sense of the news on television?	37	60	4
Can you understand more or less anything that is said to you?	30	69	1
Speaking			
Can you ask to buy something?	77	21	2
Can you cope with a visit to the doctor?	40	57	2
Can you join in a friendly informal conversation?	22	76	2
Reading			
Can you make sense of common signs?	80	18	2
Can you make sense of articles in newspapers?	41	55	4
Can you understand everything that you read?	12	87	1
Writing			
Can you write a list of words?	68	31	2
Can you string together a simple sentence?	71	27	2
Can you write about more or less anything?	12	87	1

At an advanced level, respondents felt more confident in their ability to complete the understanding (30%) and speaking (22%) tasks and less confident in their reading and writing abilities (12%).

6 Spanish

The number of adults learning Spanish in Britain is growing rapidly. Spain, and increasingly South America, as holiday destinations have led Britons to greater contact with the language. The popularity of short courses leading to basic competency is one indication of a desire to be able to 'get by' during a visit. Other factors contributing to the popularity of Spanish may be its predominance as a world language and the 'level playing field' factor whereby learning a language that has not been extensively taught in school avoids issues of prior achievement or non-achievement.

Competence in Spanish

199 of the 4,000 respondents surveyed (5%) said that they could use, understand, speak or communicate in Spanish or had learned it at some time in the past. Of these, 2 said that Spanish was their mother tongue and a further 21 said that they were bilingual in the language. The survey explored the language competence of the remaining 176.

Again only a small proportion of the 176 respondents felt confident in their ability to understand, speak, read or write fluently or very well in Spanish. However, a greater proportion felt confident in their ability to communicate in Spanish than in either French or German. Half of those who can communicate or have learned Spanish at some time in the past are confident that they can understand the language at least fairly well. 44% are confident in reading Spanish, 38% in speaking it and 26% in writing it.

Table 27: **Competence in Spanish**

	Understanding	Speaking	Reading	Writing
Base: all adults who can use, understand, speak or communicate in Spanish as a foreign language = 176 = 100%				
Fluent	2	2	2	1
Very well	5	4	5	4
Fairly well	43	32	37	21
Not very well	47	55	36	39
Not at all	3	7	20	36

Table 28 explores the competence of respondents who can understand or communicate in Spanish as a foreign language by asking them to identify whether they are able to complete specific tasks at basic, intermediate and advanced levels.

The table shows that a large proportion of respondents is successful in reaching basic level, especially in understanding (87%), speaking (82%) and reading skills (89%).

The number of respondents who can complete tasks at intermediate and advanced level falls off considerably, although still remains higher than for other languages. This fits with the popularity of short courses in Spanish which provide a 'quick fix' for holidays and the perception of Spanish being a language in which it is easy to be successful.

Table 28: **Understanding, speaking, reading and writing in Spanish**

	Yes	No	Don't know
Base: all adults who can use, understand, speak or communicate in Spanish as a foreign language = 176 = 100%			
Understanding			
Can you make sense of simple directions?	87	12	1
Can you make sense of the news on television?	44	53	3
Can you understand more or less anything that is said to you?	33	66	1
Speaking			
Can you ask to buy something?	82	17	1
Can you cope with a visit to the doctor?	52	45	2
Can you join in a friendly informal conversation?	29	70	1
Reading			
Can you make sense of common signs?	89	11	1
Can you make sense of articles in newspapers?	55	43	2
Can you understand everything that you read?	16	84	–
Writing			
Can you write a list of words?	69	29	2
Can you string together a simple sentence?	74	25	1
Can you write about more or less anything?	19	81	–

Around a third of respondents feel confident to able to complete the advanced level understanding and speaking tasks whilst only one in five feel confident in completing the advanced reading and writing tasks.

7 Italian

Having enjoyed a surge in interest some years back, the numbers of learners of Italian are now stabilising to a small but significant figure. Like Spanish the lure of taking on a language not previously tried in school is strong and the influence of cultural factors (food, music, fashion, football) should not be underestimated.

Competence in Italian

114 of the 4,000 respondents surveyed (3%) said that they could use, understand, speak or communicate in Italian or had learned it at some time in the past. Of these, 8 said that Italian was their mother tongue and a further 16 said that they were bilingual in the language. The survey explored the language competence of the remaining 90.

Like Spanish, Italian is perceived as a relatively easy language to learn, particularly for those with previous experience of French or Spanish, and learners usually become successful, very quickly. Up to 11% of the 90 respondents feel confident in their ability to understand, speak, read or write fluently or very well in Italian. This represents a greater proportion than for either Spanish, French or German. Just under half of those who can communicate or have learned Italian at some time in the past are confident that they can understand the language at least fairly well. 42% are confident in reading Italian, 34% in speaking it and just 19% in writing it.

Table 29: **Competence in Italian**

	Understanding	Speaking	Reading	Writing
Base: all adults who can use, understand, speak or communicate in Italian as a foreign language = 90 = 100%				
Fluent	3	4	2	2
Very well	6	2	9	5
Fairly well	39	28	31	12
Not very well	48	55	37	39
Not at all	4	10	21	41

Table 30 explores the competence of those respondents who can understand or communicate in Italian as a foreign language by asking them to identify whether they are able to complete specific tasks at basic, intermediate and advanced levels.

Four out of every five respondents are successful in reaching basic level in all four skills, As with other languages, the number of respondents who can complete tasks at intermediate and advanced level fall off considerably, especially with reading skills. The question concerning the intermediate writing task needs to be approached with some caution. It was originally designed to represent an intermediate level task. However, most respondents interpreted this as less complex than intended and therefore a greater proportion (71%) felt that they would be able to complete it.

Table 30: **Understanding, speaking, reading and writing in Italian**

	Yes	No	Don't know
Base: all adults who can use, understand, speak or communicate in Italian as a foreign language = 90 = 100%			
Understanding			
Can you make sense of simple directions?	85	15	–
Can you make sense of the news on television?	42	52	6
Can you understand more or less anything that is said to you?	42	58	1
Speaking			
Can you ask to buy something?	81	18	1
Can you cope with a visit to the doctor?	51	47	2
Can you join in a friendly informal conversation?	32	67	1
Reading			
Can you make sense of common signs?	81	19	–
Can you make sense of articles in newspapers?	39	51	10
Can you understand everything that you read?	21	79	–
Writing			
Can you write a list of words?	75	25	–
Can you string together a simple sentence?	71	29	–
Can you write about more or less anything?	20	80	–

Respondents are stronger in their understanding (42% confident to advanced level) and speaking skills (32% confident to advanced level) than in their reading and writing skills (one in five confident to advanced level). However, Italian is not a difficult language to read or write, and basic level skills can be achieved easily.

8 South Asian languages

Within this chapter, Hindi, Panjabi and Urdu have been combined under the label of 'South Asian' languages. A range of other languages could have also been included. However, the survey only specifically asked about these three. Additional languages of South Asian origin have been included in the following chapter – 'Other languages'.

Within Britain, this particular group of adults is unique in that it is the largest group of foreign language speakers that consistently puts their languages learned into use. Furthermore, those whose mother tongue is not English and those who are permanent residents of Great Britain are more likely to be bilingual (in their mother tongue and English) in order to participate fully in society.

Competence in South Asian languages

137 of the 4,000 respondents surveyed (3%) said that they could use, understand, speak or communicate in Hindi, Panjabi or Urdu, or had learned one or more of these at some time in the past. Of these, 46 said that one of these languages was their mother tongue and a further 18 said that they were bilingual in one of them. The survey explored the language competence of the remaining 73.

Over a half of the 73 respondents felt confident in their ability to understand and speak Hindi, Panjabi or Urdu fluently or very well. A third felt confident in their ability to read and write fluently or very well. Nearly 90% are confident that they can understand the language at least fairly well. 79% are fairly confident in speaking the languages, 49% fairly confident in reading them and 41% fairly confident in writing in them.

Table 31: **Competence in Hindi, Panjabi or Urdu**

	Understanding	Speaking	Reading	Writing
Base: all adults who can use, understand, speak or communicate in Hindi, Panjabi or Urdu as a foreign language = 73 = 100%				
Fluent	33	33	19	22
Very well	22	19	14	11
Fairly well	33	27	16	8
Not very well	8	16	19	16
Not at all	1	3	32	44

Table 32 explores the competence of those respondents who can understand or communicate in Hindi, Panjabi or Urdu as a foreign language by asking them to identify whether they are able to complete specific tasks at basic, intermediate and advanced levels. The majority of these respondents (87%) are of South Asian origin.

Both tables show a distinct difference between the level of competency in communicative skills – understanding and speaking – and skills in reading and writing. The main reason for this is that these languages are generally learned in order for respondents to be

Table 32: **Understanding, speaking, reading and writing in Hindi, Panjabi or Urdu**

	Yes	No	Don't know
Base: all adults who can use, understand, speak or communicate in Hindi, Panjabi ir Urdu as a foreign language = 73 = 100%			
Understanding			
Can you make sense of simple directions?	96	4	–
Can you make sense of the news on television?	86	14	–
Can you understand more or less anything that is said to you?	88	12	–
Speaking			
Can you ask to buy something?	82	16	–
Can you cope with a visit to the doctor?	86	12	1
Can you join in a friendly informal conversation?	75	23	–
Reading			
Can you make sense of common signs?	63	36	–
Can you make sense of articles in newspapers?	48	49	–
Can you understand everything that you read?	48	49	–
Writing			
Can you write a list of words?	52	48	–
Can you string together a simple sentence?	71	28	–
Can you write about more or less anything?	45	53	–

able to understand and communicate with others in their communities. There is therefore less need to be able to read or write in these additional languages, and thus respondents will generally only be able to do so if the language learned is of the same family as their mother tongue.

In order to maintain their cultural identity, younger generations whose primary language is English, but who have grown up in an environment where community languages are spoken, are now being taught to read and write through supplementary schools, community and religious organisations.

9 Other languages

All other languages which respondents said they could use, understand, speak or communicate in, or had learned at some time in the past are combined within this chapter. Amongst these, English, Welsh, Japanese, Portuguese and Russian were specifically asked about in the survey. However, due to the small number of respondents for each language it was impractical to deal with them separately.

- English and Welsh need to be considered separately to the other languages in this chapter, as adults in Britain generally learn them in order to be able to play a fuller part in the community in which they live and therefore require advanced levels of all four skills. The remaining languages are usually learned for different motives, affecting the level and type of skills achieved. In Tables 33-38, the data for the English and Welsh languages have been removed in order that the data is not skewed.
- Motivations for learning Japanese are frequently connected with business. Learners are often concentrated in localities where Japanese companies are based and English workers are expected to work alongside Japanese colleagues. The ethos of Japanese business often engages employees in learning about Japanese customs and culture as well as the language.
- The number of adults learning to speak Portuguese is rising, due in part to the popularity of Portugal as a holiday destination.
- Interestingly, the opening up of Russia as a business and travel destination does not seem to have encouraged new language learners, neither has the academic challenge of taking on a non-Roman script language been sustained. The expectation of previous years that Russian would become a significant world language is not fulfilled and so the language remains 'minority'.

Competence in other languages

369 of the 4,000 respondents surveyed (9%) said that they could use, understand, speak or communicate in an other language (excluding English and Welsh), or had learned one at some time in the past. Of these, 119 said that they had an other mother tongue and a further 62 said that they were bilingual in an other language. The survey explored the language competence of the remaining 188.

Table 33: **Competence in other languages**

	Understanding	Speaking	Reading	Writing
Base: all adults who can use, understand, speak or communicate in other foreign languages (excluding English and Welsh = 188 = 100%				
Fluent	8	8	4	5
Very well	9	2	9	3
Fairly well	30	27	19	11
Not very well	50	54	37	35
Not at all	2	9	31	44

Less than 20% of the 188 respondents felt confident in their ability to understand, speak, read or write fluently or very well in other languages. Respondents felt most confident in their ability to understand other languages at least fairly well (47%). 37% felt fairly confident in speaking other languages, 32% in reading other languages and only 19% in writing in other languages.

Table 34: Understanding, speaking, reading and writing in other languages

	Yes	No	Don't know
Base: all adults who can use, understand, speak or communicate in other foreign languages (excluding English and Welsh) = 188 = 100%			
Understanding			
Can you make sense of simple directions?	80	19	1
Can you make sense of the news on television?	38	60	2
Can you understand more or less anything that is said to you?	43	56	1
Speaking			
Can you ask to buy something?	74	24	1
Can you cope with a visit to the doctor?	45	54	–
Can you join in a friendly informal conversation?	35	63	2
Reading			
Can you make sense of common signs?	71	25	–4
Can you make sense of articles in newspapers?	35	60	5
Can you understand everything that you read?	16	79	5
Writing			
Can you write a list of words?	55	41	3
Can you string together a simple sentence?	59	32	4
Can you write about more or less anything?	14	84	3

Table 34 explores the competence of respondents who can understand or communicate in other foreign languages by asking them to identify whether they are able to complete specific tasks at basic, intermediate and advanced levels.

Between 70 and 80% of respondents feel confident that they can complete basic level tasks in understanding, speaking and reading, and between 35 and 45% feel confident that they can complete intermediate level tasks in these skills. In general, understanding and speaking skills are stronger than reading and writing skills, especially with languages of non-roman script.

Only 55% of respondents feel confident that they can complete a basic level writing task and the question concerning the intermediate writing task needs to be approached with some caution. The questionnaire was originally designed to represent an intermediate level task. However, most respondents interpreted this as less complex than intended and therefore a greater proportion (59%) felt that they would be able to complete it.

10 Comparative competence

In order to compare levels of competence in French, German, Spanish, Italian, South Asian and other languages (excluding English and Welsh), Tables 35-38 present the proportion of adults who can complete intermediate level tasks in understanding, speaking, reading and writing.

The survey endeavoured to encourage honesty. However, English speakers tend to underestimate their skill levels, whereas those who primarily speak community languages tend to be more realistic about their competence.

Understanding, speaking, reading and writing

Table 35 shows the proportion of adults who can make sense of the news on television in a foreign language. Although only a small number of respondents have some understanding of Hindi, Panjabi or Urdu as a foreign language, a high proportion of them (86%) feel confident to be able to make sense of the news, compared to those who have some understanding of European or other languages. French and German are understood by the greatest number of respondents. However, only a third of them said that they could make sense of the news on television.

This difference may be explained by the extent to which access to television and other media is available in these languages in Great Britain. Within South Asian culture, television and other media play a critical role in delivering information and maintaining culture, and a wide range of television and radio stations is available.

Less access exists, however, to French and German television, and even less for other languages. Limited exposure to the news on television in a foreign language may result in fewer adults feeling confident that they would be able to make sense of it.

Table 35: **Understanding – can you make sense of the news on television?**

	Base	Yes	No	Don't know
French	855	30	65	4
German	340	37	60	4
Spanish	176	44	53	3
Italian	90	42	52	6
Hindi/Panjabi/Urdu	73	86	14	–
Other (excluding English and Welsh)	188	38	60	2

Table 36 shows the proportion of adults who can cope with a visit to the doctor when speaking in a foreign language. 86% of those who are able to speak Hindi, Panjabi or Urdu as a foreign language feel confident in being able to cope, as do around a half of those who speak Spanish or Italian. Although French and German are spoken by the greatest number of respondents, only around two-fifths of them said that they could cope with a visit to the doctor. Again greater proficiency in community languages may be because coping with a visit to the doctor is a task that these respondents are required to do. Speakers of other languages may not feel so confident because they have little or no practical experience of the task.

Table 36: **Speaking – coping with a visit to the doctor**

	Base	Yes	No	Don't know
French	855	42	55	3
German	340	40	57	2
Spanish	176	52	45	2
Italian	90	51	47	2
Hindi/Panjabi/Urdu	73	86	12	1
Other (excluding English and Welsh)	188	45	54	–

Table 37: **Reading – making sense of articles in newspapers**

	Base	Yes	No	Don't know
French	855	45	52	3
German	340	42	55	4
Spanish	176	55	43	2
Italian	90	39	51	10
Hindi/Panjabi/Urdu	73	48	49	–
Other (excluding English and Welsh)	188	35	65	5

Table 37 shows the proportion of adults who can make sense of articles in newspapers when reading a foreign language. Those who read Spanish and are most confident about their ability to make sense of articles in newspapers (55%), reflecting the accessibility of the language in a written format, while only 39% of those who read Italian and 35% of readers of 'other' languages have this confidence, possibly due to limited exposure to reading materials and in the case of some 'other' languages the use of non-Roman scripts.

Respondents who can read Hindi, Panjabi or Urdu as a foreign language have much less confidence in their reading skills (48%) than in their understanding and speaking skills. This is because these languages are usually learned for communicative purposes: reading and writing are viewed as sub-skills.

Table 38: **Writing – stringing together a simple sentence**

	Base	Yes	No	Don't know
French	855	80	29	1
German	340	71	27	2
Spanish	176	74	25	1
Italian	90	71	29	–
Hindi/Panjabi/Urdu	73	71	28	–
Other (excluding English and Welsh)	188	159	32	4

Table 38 shows the proportion of adults who can string together a simple sentence when writing a foreign language. 80% of adults who can write French are confident about their ability to string together a simple sentence, compared to only 59% of adults who write 'other' languages, probably again due to the use of non-Roman scripts.

This question needs to be approached with some caution. It was originally designed to represent an intermediate level task. However, most respondents interpreted this as less complex than intended and therefore a greater proportion felt that they would be able to complete it. However, using the data collated from the basic and advanced tasks, respondents are generally less confident about their writing skills than their understanding, speaking or reading skills.

References

Carr-Hill, R., Passingham, S., Wolf, A with Kent, N. (1996) *Lost Opportunities: the language skills of linguistic minorities in England and Wales*, The Basic Skills Agency, London

Grimes, B.F. (1999) *Ethnologue: Languages of the World*, Thirteenth Edition, SIL International

Moys, A. (ed.) (1998) *Where are we going with languages?* The Nuffield Foundation, London

Sargant, N. (2000) T*he Learning Divide Revisited: a report on the findings of a UK-wide survey on adult participation in education and learning*, NIACE, Leicester

Sargant, N. with Field, J., Francis, H., Schuller, T. and Tuckett, A. (1997) *The Learning Divide: a study of participation in adult learning in the United Kingdom*, NIACE, Leicester

The Nuffield Languages Inquiry (2000) *Languages: the next generation*, The Nuffield Foundation, London

Tuckett, A. and Cara, S. (1999) *Tongue-tied but trying? A NIACE survey on the languages adults Speak in Great Britain*, NIACE, Leicester

Web-sites

www.languagelearn.co.uk	Association for Language Learning (ALL)
www.cilt.org.uk	Centre for Information on Language Teaching and Research
www.sil.org/ethnologue	Ethnologue
www.nuffieldfoundation.org/language	Nuffield Languages Inquiry
www.bwrdd-yr-iaith.org.uk	Welsh Language Board

Appendix 1: RSGB General Omnibus Survey technical appendix

The sample design, fieldwork and analysis were carried out by RSGB (Research Surveys of Great Britain), who have provided the following description of the survey method.

Method

The data presented was obtained as part of the RSGB's General Omnibus Survey for April 1999. Appendix 6 contains a copy of the questionnaire.

Sample

The survey was based on a representative sample of 4000 adults i.e. males and females aged 16 or over. They were selected from a minimum of 260 sampling points by a random location method.

Fieldwork

Respondents were interviewed at home organised by SFR's Regional Managers according to RSGB's detailed instructions about the survey and administration procedures.

The interviews took place during the periods 28 April – 2 May and 5 – 9 May 1999.

Data processing

After coding and editing the data, weights were used to allow for sampling variation. The weighting scheme took account of the boost interviews by weighting the boosted regions back to their normal proportion of the Great Britain populations. Details of the weights and unweighted sample are shown in Appendix 5.

Appendix 2: Notes on the tables

Figures in the tables are from the 1999 RSGB/NIACE survey unless otherwise indicated.

Tables are percentaged vertically unless otherwise specified.

All tables are based on weighted totals. Researchers who wish to pursue any particular topic can obtain the necessary basic figures from the set of full analyses at NIACE.

In tables, * indicates less than 0.5% but greater than zero, and – indicates zero.

Percentages equal to or greater than 0.5 have been rounded up in all tables (e.g. 0.5 per cent = one per cent, 36.5 per cent = 37 per cent)

Owing to the effects of rounding weighted data, the weighted bases shown in the tables may not always add up to the expected base.

In a number of questions, respondents were invited to give more than one answer: and so percentages may well add to more than 100%.

Some sub-questions are filtered, that is, they are only asked of a proportion of respondents. Where questions are filtered, the base of the relevant group is indicated at the beginning of that table and percentages are derived from that base.

Regional analyses: inevitably, the number of sampling points in any one region is small – on average, one for every ten interviews. This fact should be taken into account when interpreting regional differences.

Appendix 3: A guide to socio-economic class

Grade 'A' households: the upper middle class
Informants from Grade 'A' households constitute about 3% of the total. The head of the household is a successful business or professional person, senior civil servant, or has considerable private means. A young person in some of these occupations who is not yet fully established may still be found in Grade 'B', though s/he eventually should reach Grade 'A'. In country or suburban areas, 'A' grade households usually live in large detached houses or in expensive flats. In towns, they may live in expensive flats or town houses in better parts of town.

Grade 'B' households: the middle class
Grade 'B' informants account for about 10% of the total. In general, the heads of 'B' grade households will be quite senior people but not at the very top of their profession or business. They are quite well-off, but their style of life is generally respectable rather than rich or luxurious. Non-earners will be living on private pensions or on fairly modest private means.

Grade 'C1' households: the lower middle class
Grade 'C1' constitutes about 24% of total informants. In general it is made up of families of small tradespeople and non-manual workers who carry out less important administrative, supervisory and clerical jobs i.e. what are sometimes called 'white collar' workers.

Grade 'C2' households: the skilled working class
Grade 'C2' consists in the main of skilled manual workers and their families. It constitutes about 30% of informants. When in doubt as to whether the head of the household is skilled or unskilled, check whether s/he has served an apprenticeship; this may be a guide, though not all skilled workers have served an apprenticeship.

Grade 'D' households: the semi-skilled and unskilled working class
Grade 'D' consists of entirely manual workers, generally semi-skilled or unskilled. This grade accounts for 25% of families. It also includes non-earners: retired people who before retirement would have been in Grade 'D' and have pensions other than State Pensions, or have other private means.

Grade 'E' households: those at lowest levels of subsistence
Grade 'E' consists of old age pensioners, widows and their families, casual workers and those who, through sickness and employment, are dependent upon social security schemes. They constitute about 8% of all informants.

Appendix 4: Regions

London:	Outer and Inner London Boroughs
South East:	Bedfordshire, Berkshire, Buckinghamshire, East Sussex, Hampshire, Hertfordshire, Kent, Surrey, West Sussex
South West:	Avon, Cornwall, Devon, Dorset, Gloucestershire, Somerset, Wiltshire.
East Anglia:	Cambridgeshire, Norfolk, Suffolk.
East Midlands:	Derbyshire, Leicestershire, Lincolnshire, Northamptonshire, Nottinghamshire.
West Midlands:	Hereford and Worcester, Shropshire, Staffordshire, Warwickshire, West Midlands.
North West:	Cheshire, Greater Manchester, Lancashire, Merseyside.
Yorkshire/Humberside:	Humberside, North Yorkshire, South Yorkshire, West Yorkshire.
The North:	Cleveland, Cumbria, Durham, Northumberland, Tyne and Wear.
Wales:	All counties.
Scotland:	All counties.

Appendix 5: Analysis of weighted and unweighted samples

Base: all respondents	Weighted		Unweighted	
All	4,000	100%	3,967	100%
Gender				
Men	1,870	47	1,650	42
Women	2,130	53	2,317	58
Age				
16-24	524	13	547	14
25-34	729	18	804	20
35-44	735	18	791	20
45-54	669	17	588	15
55+	1,343	34	1,237	31
Class				
AB	644	16	550	14
C1	1,173	29	1,033	26
C2	897	22	861	22
DE	1,286	32	1,523	38
Working status				
Full-time	1,513	38	1,388	35
Part-time (8-29 hours)	497	12	540	14
Part-time (under 8 hours)	42	1	46	1
Retired	1,006	25	931	23
Still at school	62	2	53	1
Full-time higher education	157	4	157	4
Unemployed (seeking)	169	4	185	5
Unemployed (not seeking)	554	14	667	17
Male chief income earner	2,531	63	2,445	62
Female chief income earner	1,015	25	1,111	28
Male main shopper	859	21	760	19
Female main shopper	1,770	44	2,081	52
Household size				
1	739	18	723	18
2	1,376	34	1,313	33
3	717	18	725	18
4	718	18	730	18
5	326	8	344	9
6	88	2	96	2
7	25	1	25	1
8	9	*	8	*
9	3	*	2	*
10+	1	*	1	*
Standard region				
Yorkshire and Humberside	352	9	332	8
North	216	5	257	6
South West	340	8	338	9
East Midlands	288	7	303	8
South East	776	19	698	18
East Anglia	148	4	158	4
West Midlands	372	9	393	10
North West	452	11	420	11
Wales	204	5	212	5
Scotland	360	9	360	9
London	492	12	496	13

Appendix 6: The questionnaire

Do not show screen until told to do so

Q1. What is your mother tongue, that is the language you first learned as a child?

Scripter: do not rotate

01 English
02 French
03 German
04 Hindi
05 Italian
06 Japanese
07 Portuguese
08 Panjabi
09 Russian
10 Spanish
11 Urdu
12 Welsh
13 Other (type in) _____
(Don't know)

Q2. Are you bilingual at all?

Interviewer: if yes, probe for other main language

01 English
02 French
03 German
04 Hindi
05 Italian
06 Japanese
07 Portuguese
08 Panjabi
09 Russian
10 Spanish
11 Urdu
12 Welsh
13 Other (type in) _____
(No)
(Don't know)

Multi choice

Q.3 Are there any other languages that you can use or understand, speak or communicate, or have learned at any time in the past?

Interviewer: If yes, probe for other languages

01 English
02 French
03 German
04 Hindi
05 Italian
06 Japanese
07 Portuguese
08 Panjabi
09 Russian
10 Spanish
11 Urdu
12 Welsh
13 Other (type in) _____
(Don't know)

Ask Q. 4-7 for each language coded at Q.3 all others to Q.8

The next few questions are all to do with your general understanding of (language at Q.3)

Show screen

Q.4a How well do you understand (language at Q.3)?

01 Fluent
02 Very well
03 Fairly well
04 Not very well
05 Not at all well
(Don't know)

Q.4b Can you make sense of simple directions?

01 Yes
02 No
(Don't know)

Q.4c Can you make sense of the news on television?

01 Yes
02 No
(Don't know)

Q.4d Can you understand more or less anything that is said to you?

01 Yes
02 No
(Don't know)
Show screen

Q.5a How well do you speak (language at Q.3)

01 Fluent
02 Very well
03 Fairly well
04 Not very well
05 Not at all
(Don't know)

Q.5b When speaking (language at Q.3), can you join in a friendly informal conversation without any difficulty?

01 Yes
02 No
(Don't know)

Q.5c Can you ask to buy something is (language at Q.3)?

01 Yes
02 No
(Don't know)

Q.5d Could you cope with a visit to the doctors?

01 Yes
02 No
(Don't know)

Show screen

Q.6a And how well do you read (language at Q.3)?

01 Fluent
02 Very well
03 Fairly well
04 Not very well
05 Not at all
(Don't know)

Q.6b Can you understand everything that you read?

01 Yes
02 No
(Don't know)

Q.6c Can you make sense of common signs?

01 Yes
02 No
(Don't know)

Q.6d Can you make sense of articles in newspapers and magazines?

01 Yes
02 No
(Don't know)

Show screen

Q.7a And how well do you write (language at Q.3)?

01 Fluent
02 Very well
03 Fairly well
04 Not very well
05 Not at all
(Don't know)

Q.7b Can you write a list of words?

01 Yes
02 No
(Don't know)

Q.7c Can you string together a simple sentence?

01 Yes
02 No
(Don't know)

Q.7d can you write about more or less anything you want?

01 Yes
02 No
(Don't know)

Do not show the screen until told to do so

Multi choice

Q.8 Are you currently learning any languages?

Interviewer: If yes, probe for which ones

01 English
02 French
03 German
04 Hindi
05 Italian
06 Japanese
07 Portuguese
08 Panjabi
09 Russian
10 Spanish
11 Urdu
12 Welsh
13 Other (type in) _____
(No)
(Don't know)

Multi choice

Q.9 Are there any languages you would like to learn if you had the time and opportunity?

Interviewer: If yes, probe for which ones

01 English
02 French
03 German
04 Hindi
05 Italian
06 Japanese
07 Portuguese
08 Panjabi
09 Russian
10 Spanish
11 Urdu
12 Welsh
13 Other (type in) _____
(No)
(Don't know)

Show screen

Q.10 Could you please tell which of the following best describes your ethnic group?

01 White
02 Black – Caribbean
03 Black – African
04 Black – British
05 Black – Other (specify)
06 Bangladeshi
07 Indian
08 Pakistani
09 Chinese
10 Asian – British
11 Asian – Other (specify)
12 Arab
13 Cypriot
14 Other (specify)
Don't know